ANTA...
Race to the South Pole

by Cynthia Benjamin • illustrated by Berney Knox

Chapters

Harcourt

Orlando   Boston   Dallas   Chicago   San Diego

Visit *The Learning Site!*

www.harcourtschool.com

Antarctica: Land of Mystery

Because Antarctica is so far from the rest of the world, it has always been thought of as a land of mystery. Although they never saw it, the ancient Greeks always believed there was a great southern continent covered by ice. Later, maps called land in this part of the world "The Unknown Southern Land." A lot has changed since then!

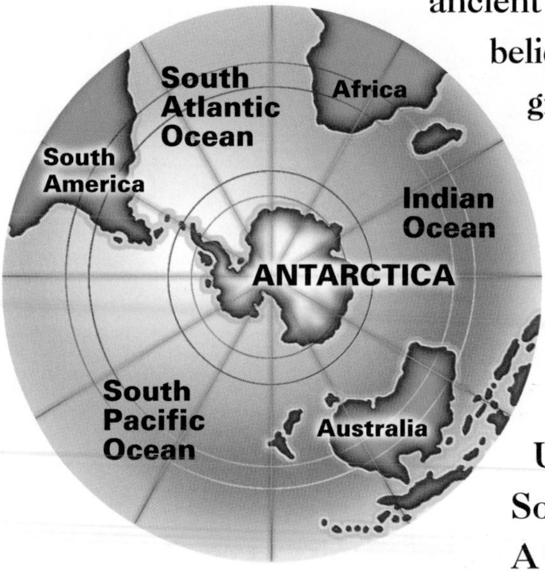

Map showing Antarctica and surrounding oceans

We now know that Antarctica is a very cold continent. It's covered by a layer of ice about 7,100 feet thick. The temperature there hardly ever reaches higher than 32° Fahrenheit (0° C). The winter months are from May to August. In the winter it can get as cold as -94° Fahrenheit! The icy winds make it feel even colder.

Ships traveling to Antarctica face a perilous trip around icebergs and piles of ice. When the passengers arrive, they see that thick ice covers the land. This thick layer of ice and snow is called the Antarctic icecap. It covers 98 percent of Antarctica. Beneath this blanket of ice are mountains, lowlands, and valleys.

The Transantarctic Mountains divide Antarctica into two large areas. They are called East Antarctica and West Antarctica. The South Pole is in East Antarctica.

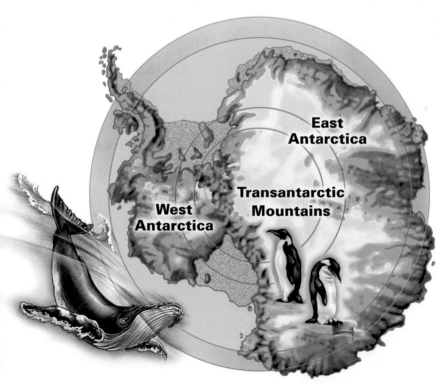

East
Antarctica

Transantarctic
Mountains

West
Antarctica

Early Explorers

For hundreds of years, people believed that a very hot region surrounded the equator and blocked the way south, making it impassable. For this reason, no one explored Antarctica.

Finally, in 1772, James Cook began his search for a southern continent. He was told by the British navy to sail as far south as possible. He

crossed the Antarctic Circle in 1773, but huge blocks of ice kept him from continuing. He never saw land.

In 1823 James Weddell traveled south looking for seals to hunt. He sailed farther south than anyone had before.

**James Cook,
British explorer**

About 1840, Charles Wilkes explored the coast of Antarctica. He proved that the land was large enough to be called a continent.

In 1895 Henryk Johan Bull and his whaling crew were the first people to land on Antarctica. However, the first inland exploration of Antarctica didn't take place until the early 1900s.

Ernest Shackleton, Antarctic explorer

Between 1901 and 1904 Robert Scott led an expedition to the Ross Sea. A group from this expedition got as far as the edge of the inland plateau, where the South Pole is located. In 1907 a member of Scott's team returned to Antarctica. Ernest Shackleton came within 97 miles of the South Pole.

Exploring Antarctica by Air

In the twentieth century, people began to explore Antarctica by air. In 1928 Sir Hubert Wilking became the first person to fly over Antarctic land. This Australian explorer saw the Antarctic Peninsula and nearby islands.

Richard E. Byrd flew over the South Pole in 1929.

A year later, Richard E. Byrd, a U.S. naval officer, led the first flight over the South Pole. The journey lasted less than sixteen hours. It was part of a two-year expedition to study the icecap, the weather, and the geology there.

Almost twenty years later, Byrd led another expedition called Operation Highjump. This was the largest Antarctic expedition by a single country. The group discovered new land and photographed a part of the coast that had never been explored before.

The Race to the South Pole

The Importance of Reaching the South Pole

For centuries adventurers have set out on voyages of exploration to learn more about the world. By 1909, there was only one unexplored area left in the world: the South Pole.

Amundsen's route through the Northwest Passage

Two explorers, Roald Amundsen and Robert Scott, set out to reach it. Which man would be the first to reach this last remaining prize?

Roald Amundsen

Early Life and First Explorations

Roald Amundsen was born in Norway in 1872. He was the son of a ship captain. He grew up in an area with cold, stormy winters. It was the perfect childhood for a future Antarctic explorer. As a child, young Roald read the words of the polar explorer Sir John Franklin and decided to become a polar explorer, too.

Amundsen set out to achieve his goal. He trained hard to make himself strong. He went to school to learn seamanship. Then he joined the crew of the *Belgica*. This ship set sail for Antarctica in August 1897.

**Roald Amundsen,
Norwegian explorer
(1872–1928)**

The Next Great Adventure

When Amundsen got back from this grueling expedition, he finished his sea training. By April 1900, he was ready to lead his own expedition.

Amundsen wanted to sail through the Northwest Passage. On June 16, 1903, Amundsen and his crew left for the Arctic on the *Gjoa*.

Amundsen had learned a great deal from his experience on the *Belgica*. He knew it was important to take good care of his crew. He made sure his men had a healthy diet and ate fresh, not rancid, meat. There was always enough water so the crew wouldn't suffer from dehydration.

His expedition was a success! In 1906 Amundsen's ship became the first to travel through the Northwest Passage. What would be next?

The Race Begins

Getting Ready

Roald Amundsen's trip through the Northwest Passage made him a world-famous explorer. As soon as he returned, he began raising money to pay for his next great adventure.

Another famous Norwegian explorer loaned Amundsen his ship, the *Fram*. The plan was to prepare the *Fram* for a seven-year trip that would begin in early 1910.

Amundsen planned to sail around the tip of South America and then go on to San Francisco, to Alaska, and into the polar sea. However, just before he left Norway, he heard upsetting news. Two other explorers, Frederick Cook and Robert Peary, both said that they had reached the North Pole. Amundsen didn't want to repeat their success. Now he had to come up with a new plan.

Amundsen's ship, the *Fram*

10

The crew of the *Fram*

A Change in Plans

Amundsen decided to become the first explorer to reach the South Pole instead. At the same time, Robert Scott was also getting ready to reach the South Pole. When Amundsen found out about Scott's plans, he decided to try to beat him there.

Amundsen carefully chose a crew and bought sled dogs for the journey. All the while he kept his real goal a secret—even from his sailors. When the *Fram* stopped at an island for repairs, Amundsen finally told the sailors their real destination. He gave all of them the chance to leave the ship and return home. None of them did.

Next, Amundsen told Scott the *Fram's* true goal. The race to the South Pole had started!

The Polar Journey

The *Fram* was a good ship. It arrived at the Bay of Whales on the Ross Ice Shelf on January 5, 1911. Crews on other ships had to bail water during storms. However, the men on the *Fram* never had that problem.

Amundsen and his crew used the next few months to set up their winter camp. It was called Framheim. Amundsen selected the location for the camp because it was 60 miles closer to the pole than Robert Scott's base camp. While some men set up a wooden building where they would live, others went hunting. Amundsen knew it was important for his crew to have fresh meat to stay healthy.

Indian Ocean

ANTARCTICA
Ross Ice
Shelf

Atlantic
Ocean

Bay of
Whales
Camp

Pacific
Ocean

Antarctic
Circle

While they worked, Amundsen worried about Scott's plans. He had heard that Robert Scott was using new sleds with motors. In fact, Scott's modern sleds kept breaking down and weren't useful.

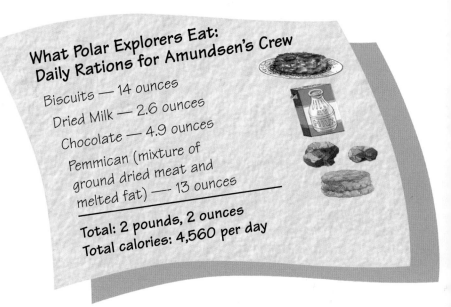

What Polar Explorers Eat:
Daily Rations for Amundsen's Crew

Biscuits — 14 ounces
Dried Milk — 2.6 ounces
Chocolate — 4.9 ounces
Pemmican (mixture of
ground dried meat and
melted fat) — 13 ounces

Total: 2 pounds, 2 ounces
Total calories: 4,560 per day

Amundsen and his men spent the winter in their warm and comfortable wooden home. Outside, the cold wind roared across the thick ice like a hungry lion. The men were busy getting ready for their South Pole journey. It would begin in the spring.

It was important to leave food along the route they would follow. They used strong dogs to help them. Amundsen called these dogs "our children."

The sled dogs worked hard. They helped the men set up seven areas with food. Now the men waited for spring so they could start for the South Pole.

Victory!

Amundsen and four of his men set out for the South Pole on October 19, 1911. Thirteen dogs pulled each sled. It was hard to travel when they reached the high mountains. The men helped the dogs pull the sleds over the ice and snow.

Next, they faced blizzards. However, the men wouldn't give up and finally reached the Polar Plateau.

Now the trip became easier. They made good progress across the Antarctic landscape. The men set up a last area for food about 95 miles from the South Pole. They marked it with a line of black poles. This would help them find it on the way back.

Reaching the Goal

There was only one remaining problem. They still didn't know if Robert Scott and his team had beaten them to the prize.

As the tired men approached the pole, Amundsen took the lead. On December 14, 1911, Roald Amundsen reached what he believed was the South Pole.

Everyone shook hands as Amundsen planted the Norwegian flag in the snow. The team stayed at that camp for three days. In a small tent there, Amundsen left letters to Robert Scott and the King of Norway. If he didn't survive the return trip, he wanted Scott to deliver the letter to the King to confirm his achievement.

Not long after that, the Norwegians realized that they had missed the exact location of the South Pole by about five miles. On December 17, 1911, they set out for the actual pole and reached it. Amundsen had achieved his goal. He was the first person to reach the South Pole!

Antarctica Today

Today, Antarctica is a center of important scientific research. More than thirty scientific stations are located there, and they are open all year round. They are run by many countries, including the United States, Australia, Great Britain, and Japan.

In the summer, scientists collect rocks from valleys of the Transantarctic Mountains. They also study Antarctic animals, such as whales and seals. During the winter, they study earthquakes and record information about the weather. Other scientists are trying to find out why the layer of ozone, a form of oxygen, is becoming thinner above Antarctica.